Storyline

THE JOURNAL

Storyline: The Journal
Copyright © 2018 by Kay Moorby

Soulwithaview Media Ltd
Rotherham
S63 6ER

Unless otherwise indicated, all Scripture quotations are taken from the Holy Bible, New Living Translation, copyright © 1996, 2004, 2007, 2013, 2015 by Tyndale House Foundation. Used by permission of Tyndale House Publishers, Inc., Carol Stream, Illinois 60188. All rights reserved.

Scripture quotations marked MSG are taken from THE MESSAGE, copyright © 1993, 1994, 1995, 1996, 2000, 2001, 2002 by Eugene H. Peterson. Used by permission of NavPress. All rights reserved. Represented by Tyndale House Publishers, Inc.

Contemporary English Version, Second Edition (CEV®)
© 2006 American Bible Society. All rights reserved.

Anglicisations © British and Foreign Bible Society 1997. The copyright for the derivative work of Anglicisation pertains only to the text within the Contemporary English Version (CEV) that British and Foreign Bible Society adapted for British literary usage, consistent with Section 103(b) of the United States Copyright Act, 17 U.S.C. § 103(b).

Bible text from the Contemporary English Version 2nd Edition (CEV®) is not to be reproduced in copies or otherwise by any means except as permitted in writing by American Bible Society, 101 North Independence Mall East, Floor 8, Philadelphia, PA 19106-2155 (www.americanbible.org).

All rights reserved. No part of this publication may be reproduced, stored in a retrieval system, or transmitted in any form or by any means - electronic, mechanical, photocopy, recording, or any other - except for brief quotations in printed reviews, without the prior permission of the publisher.

Icon design by Nina Hunter

Design by Kay Moorby & More Than Just Design (www.morethanjustdesign.co.uk)

ISBN 978-09-56745-22-4

Storyline

What have been the twists and turns of your story so far?
Who is writing your story?

Storylines are rarely linear and often complex. They feature plot twists, adventure, heartache and excitement. Their characters face adversity, journey with friends and overcome their deepest fears. The storylines of the books that line our shelves are often polished and carefully thought through, but real life isn't always like that. With so many options we can struggle to decide which storyline to follow.

Dotted throughout the complex storyline of Jesus lies a wealth of simple stories. Tales of lost sheep, praying widows and self-important Pharisees. To comprehend their meaning, you will require open eyes, listening ears and a heart ready to understand.

The Storyline Journal provides space for personal reflection and note-taking. It also contains many of the key discussion quotes, questions and key scripture covered in each session.

Storyline

Storyline
THE JOURNAL

CONTENTS

Lub Dub..7-23
The condition of the heart

Blot..25-39
The power of grace and forgiveness

Kerching...41-53
The cost of discipleship

Tic Toc..55-69
The way we invest our time and talents

Tweet..71-87
The importance of prayer

Glug..89-100
The capacity for change

Lub Dub

Lub Dub

Lub Dub

Jesus looked out at the expansive crowd gathered before Him.
Why had they come to listen?
Dragged along by a friend?
Searching for answers?
Thirsty for more?
Each heart came with a different need, question and willingness to listen. We will never know the backstory of the crowd that gathered there that day, or the impact the words of Jesus would have on their heart. Some would never think of Jesus again, others would dedicate their lives to Him.
The only difference was the condition of their heart.

Today's Special

"And I will give you a new heart, and I will put a new spirit in you. I will take out your stony, stubborn heart and give you a tender, responsive heart."

Ezekiel 36:26

The Condition of the Heart
Jesus Tells the Parable of the Four Soils

Matthew 13:1-23

¹ Later that same day Jesus left the house and sat beside the lake. ² A large crowd soon gathered around him, so he got into a boat. Then he sat there and taught as the people stood on the shore. ³ He told many stories in the form of parables, such as this one:

"Listen! A farmer went out to plant some seeds. ⁴ As he scattered them across his field, some seeds fell on a footpath, and the birds came and ate them. ⁵ Other seeds fell on shallow soil with underlying rock. The seeds sprouted quickly because the soil was shallow. ⁶ But the plants soon wilted under the hot sun, and since they didn't have deep roots, they died. ⁷ Other seeds fell among thorns that grew up and choked out the tender plants. ⁸ Still other seeds fell on fertile soil, and they produced a crop that was thirty, sixty, and even a hundred times as much as had been planted! ⁹ Anyone with ears to hear should listen and understand."

¹⁰ His disciples came and asked him, "Why do you use parables when you talk to the people?"

¹¹ He replied, "You are permitted to understand the secrets of the Kingdom of Heaven, but others are not. ¹² To those who listen to my teaching, more understanding will be given, and they will have an abundance of knowledge. But for those who are not listening, even what little understanding they have will be taken away from them. ¹³ That is why I use these parables,

For they look, but they don't really see.
    They hear, but they don't really listen or understand.

¹⁴ This fulfills the prophecy of Isaiah that says, 'When you hear what I say, you will not understand. When you see what I do, you will not comprehend. ¹⁵ For the hearts of these people are hardened, and their ears cannot hear, and they have closed their eyes— so their eyes cannot see, and their ears cannot hear, and their hearts cannot understand, and they cannot turn to me and let me heal them.' ¹⁶ "But blessed are your eyes, because they see; and your ears, because they hear. ¹⁷ I tell you the truth, many prophets and righteous people longed to see what you see, but they didn't see it. And they longed to hear what you hear, but they didn't hear it.

¹⁸ "Now listen to the explanation of the parable about the farmer planting seeds: ¹⁹ The seed that fell on the footpath represents those who hear the message about the Kingdom and don't understand it. Then the evil one comes and snatches away the seed that was planted in their hearts. ²⁰ The seed on the rocky soil represents those who hear the message and immediately receive it with joy. ²¹ But since they don't have deep roots, they don't last long. They fall away as soon as they have problems or are persecuted for believing God's word.

²² The seed that fell among the thorns represents those who hear God's word, but all too quickly the message is crowded out by the worries of this life and the lure of wealth, so no fruit is produced. ²³ The seed that fell on good soil represents those who truly hear and understand God's word and produce a harvest of thirty, sixty, or even a hundred times as much as had been planted!"

Four Types of Soil

Roadside

The roadside referred to the network of dried out pathways that formed the edges of the farmer's field. As the farmer scattered the seed, it was likely that some would fall on the hardened walkways alongside the lush soil. It was impossible for these seeds to survive as they were left exposed on the surface and were reduced to bird feed.

Rock

When we think of the rock soil, we may be tempted to picture a field full of rocks but an experienced farmer would not have scattered seed on soil like this. Above the surface the soil would have looked perfectly good for planting, but underneath there would have been a layer of rock stopping the roots from growing.

Thorns

At first glance, the ploughed field would have looked no different to any other soil ready for planting, but hidden away the thorns were waiting to grow. As the healthy plants started to flourish then the thorns crowded around them, competing for nutrients, water and a place in the sun. Suffocated by the thorns, the healthy plants would have their growth stunted and eventually die.

Fertile

The ideal soil for planting is deep soil, free from weeds, full of nutrients and freshly ploughed. Soil in this condition will take in seeds and help them to flourish, generating a significant return for the farmer.

Four Types of Soil

Roadside

Rock

Thorns

Fertile

Lub Dub

The same seeds are used in all four soils and are scattered in the same way, by the same farmer.

Imagine that each heart described in the parable is represented by a real person. What would their everyday life be like?

Matters of the Heart

Reflect on the following Bible verses about the condition of the heart.

Proverbs 4:23

Proverbs 27:19

Jeremiah 29:13

Matthew 22:37

Psalm 19:14

Psalm 31:24

After reflecting on these Bible verses, what have you discovered about the importance of the condition of our heart?

Lub Dub

"Search me, O God, and know my heart; test me and know my anxious thoughts. Point out anything in me that offends you, and lead me along the path of everlasting life."
Psalm 139:23-24

"In short, Jesus' parables has a clear twofold purpose: They hid the truth from self-righteous or self-satisfied people who fancied themselves too sophisticated to learn from Him, while the same parables revealed truth to eager souls with childlike faith - those who were hungering and thirsty for righteousness."
(John Macarthur, 2016)

"Blessed are the pure in heart, for they will see God."
Matthew 5:8

Father,
I want to be ready for You,
for what you have to teach me and all I can be in You.
If my heart is hard, deaf to Your word through sadness,
hurt or selfishness - soften me.
If my heart is shallow, ready to give up when things get hard - feed me.
If my heart is threatened or distracted by worry,
fear or reward - help me to trust you.
Lord, renew my heart and fill it full of Your Holy Spirit.
Make it loving, joyful, peaceful, patient, kind, good,
faithful, gentle and with self-control - so I can be all these things to others.
(Alex Mortimer, 2017)

Thirsty?

The following music tracks can be used to provide additional refreshment during your meal.
King of My Heart - Piano Prayer
Open the Eyes of My Heart Lord - Shane and Shane

Blot

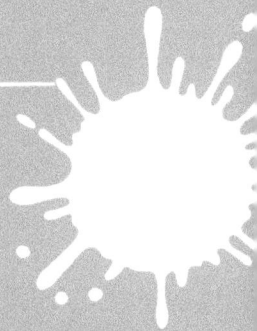

Blot

Blot

Holding on tightly to the jar of perfume, she made her way across the room to Jesus. She must have known what they thought of her. As her tears mingled with the expensive scent and she dried the feet of Jesus with her hair, she must have sensed the looks of disgust from Simon the Pharisee. He had barely offered Jesus a drink let alone washed His feet. Why was Jesus letting this woman touch him? Responding to Simon, Jesus said:
"I tell you, her sins - and there are many - have been forgiven, so she has shown me much love. But a person who is forgiven little shows only little love."
As she washed away the dirt from Jesus' feet, her faith and His forgiveness blotted out every stain.

Today's Special

"But when God our Saviour revealed his kindness and love, he saved us, not because of the righteous things we had done, but because of His mercy. He washed away our sins, giving us a new birth and new life through the Holy Spirit."

Titus 3:4-5

The Power of Grace & Forgiveness
Jesus Anointed by a Sinful Woman

Luke 7:36-50

36 One of the Pharisees asked Jesus to have dinner with him, so Jesus went to his home and sat down to eat. 37 When a certain immoral woman from that city heard he was eating there, she brought a beautiful alabaster jar filled with expensive perfume. 38 Then she knelt behind him at his feet, weeping. Her tears fell on his feet, and she wiped them off with her hair. Then she kept kissing his feet and putting perfume on them.
39 When the Pharisee who had invited him saw this, he said to himself, "If this man were a prophet, he would know what kind of woman is touching him. She's a sinner!"
40 Then Jesus answered his thoughts. "Simon," he said to the Pharisee, "I have something to say to you."
"Go ahead, Teacher," Simon replied.

41 Then Jesus told him this story: "A man loaned money to two people—500 pieces of silver to one and 50 pieces to the other. 42 But neither of them could repay him, so he kindly forgave them both, cancelling their debts. Who do you suppose loved him more after that?"

43 Simon answered, "I suppose the one for whom he cancelled the larger debt."
"That's right," Jesus said. 44 Then he turned to the woman and said to Simon, "Look at this woman kneeling here. When I entered your home, you didn't offer me water to wash the dust from my feet, but she has washed them with her tears and wiped them with her hair. 45 You didn't greet me with a kiss, but

from the time I first came in, she has not stopped kissing my feet. [46] You neglected the courtesy of olive oil to anoint my head, but she has anointed my feet with rare perfume. [47] "I tell you, her sins—and they are many—have been forgiven, so she has shown me much love. But a person who is forgiven little shows only little love." [48] Then Jesus said to the woman, "Your sins are forgiven." [49] The men at the table said among themselves, "Who is this man, that he goes around forgiving sins?" [50] And Jesus said to the woman, "Your faith has saved you; go in peace."

Jesus Warns Against Looking Down on Others

Matthew 18:10-14

[10] "Beware that you don't look down on any of these little ones. For I tell you that in heaven their angels are always in the presence of my heavenly Father. [12] "If a man has a hundred sheep and one of them wanders away, what will he do? Won't he leave the ninety-nine others on the hills and go out to search for the one that is lost? [13] And if he finds it, I tell you the truth, he will rejoice over it more than over the ninety-nine that didn't wander away! [14] In the same way, it is not my heavenly Father's will that even one of these little ones should perish.

Jesus Tells the Parable of the Unforgiving Debtor

Matthew 18:21-35

[21] Then Peter came to him and asked, "Lord, how often should I forgive someone who sins against me? Seven times?" [22] "No, not seven times," Jesus replied, "but seventy times seven! [23] "Therefore, the Kingdom of Heaven can be compared to a king who decided to bring his accounts up to date with servants who had borrowed money from him. [24] In the process, one of his debtors was brought in who owed him millions of dollars. [25] He couldn't pay, so his master ordered that he be sold—along with his wife, his children, and everything he owned—to pay the debt. [26] "But the man fell down before his master and begged him, 'Please, be patient with me, and I will pay it all.' [27] Then his master was filled with pity for him, and he released him and forgave his debt.

[28] "But when the man left the king, he went to a fellow servant who owed him a few thousand dollars. He grabbed him by the throat and demanded instant payment.

[29] "His fellow servant fell down before him and begged for a little more time. 'Be patient with me, and I will pay it,' he pleaded. [30] But his creditor wouldn't wait. He had the man arrested and put in prison until the debt could be paid in full.

[31] "When some of the other servants saw this, they were very upset. They went to the king and told him everything that had happened. [32] Then the king called in the man he had forgiven and said, 'You evil servant! I forgave you that tremendous debt because you pleaded with me. [33] Shouldn't you have mercy on your fellow servant, just as I had mercy on you?' [34] Then the angry king sent the

man to prison to be tortured until he had paid his entire debt. ³⁵ "That's what my heavenly Father will do to you if you refuse to forgive your brothers and sisters from your heart."

....

....

....

....

....

"Everyone thinks forgiveness is a lovely idea until he has something to forgive."
(C.S. Lewis, 1952)

Blot

"Forgiveness and a restoration of a relationship are two different things. Forgiveness is only on your part, whether they respond or not, whether they ask for it or not, whether they even recognise it or not. You forgive for your sake. Restoration of a relationship takes far more than forgiveness. It takes repentance. It takes restitution and a rebuilding of trust. And it often takes a much longer time."
(Rick Warren, 2014)

Others

Discuss the following quote.

"Stress says that the things we are involved in are important enough to merit our impatience, our lack of grace toward others, or our tight grip of control."
(Francis Chan & Danae Yankoski, 2012)

Can you think of a time where you showed a lack of grace to someone else? Describe what happened.

If you are honest with yourself then what was the reason behind that?

In what ways do we justify showing a lack of grace to others?

Gossip

What does the book of Proverbs have to say about gossip?

Proverbs 10:18
"Hiding hatred makes you a liar; slandering others makes you a fool."

Proverbs 11:13
"A gossip goes around telling secrets, but those who are trustworthy can keep a confidence."

Proverbs 15:1
"A gentle answer deflects anger, but harsh words make tempers flare."

Proverbs 17:9
"Love prospers when a fault is forgiven, but dwelling on it separates close friends."

Proverbs 20:19
"A gossip goes around telling secrets, so don't hang around with chatterers."

Proverbs 26:20
"Fire goes out without wood, and quarrels disappear when gossip stops."

What have you learned about the importance of not gossiping about others and how to deal with those who gossip about you?

How will it change the way that you deal with gossip?

Blot

What have you learned about grace and forgiveness during this session?
How will what you have discovered change your storyline in the future?

'Love.....keeps no record of wrongs'
1 Corinthians 13:5

Jesus, how many times have I come to You to be forgiven? Too many!
You are Almighty God and have died on the cross for me and still I
fall short and come back again and again asking for more of your
mercy and grace.
Yet You welcome me each and every time. Amazing!
You open Your arms and tell me I am a Child of a King!
So help me Lord to show that same forgiveness to others. It doesn't make
me weak; it's not 'giving in'. It doesn't make me better than anyone else.
It's about loving and living Your way. It's knowing that You have done
so much for me and that I must try to do the same to others,
even when it is difficult.
(Alex Mortimer, 2017)

Thirsty?

The following music tracks can be used to provide additional refreshment during your meal.
Mercy - Brave New World
Every Mile Mattered - Nichole Nordeman

Kerching

Kerching

Kerching

Surrounded by blueprints, bank statements and spreadsheets the entrepreneur scanned the plans for the biggest building project he had ever undertaken. Every possible calculation had been made and every financial option explored. Despite the meticulous planning, this was going to take every single penny he had, but he knew it would be worth it.

Let's be straight, Jesus asks for everything! It's up to us whether, after counting the cost, we choose to follow Him. A life of discipleship costs us everything but it leads to a lifelong investment in a building project that is beyond anything we could dream or imagine.

Today's Special

"Now all glory to God, who is able, through his mighty power at work in us, to accomplish infinitely more than we might ask or think."
Ephesians 3:20

The Cost of Discipleship
Jesus Teaches About the Cost of Being a Disciple

Luke 14:28-33

²⁸ "But don't begin until you count the cost. For who would begin construction of a building without first calculating the cost to see if there is enough money to finish it? ²⁹ Otherwise, you might complete only the foundation before running out of money, and then everyone would laugh at you. ³⁰ They would say, 'There's the person who started that building and couldn't afford to finish it!' ³¹ "Or what king would go to war against another king without first sitting down with his counsellors to discuss whether his army of 10,000 could defeat the 20,000 soldiers marching against him? ³² And if he can't, he will send a delegation to discuss terms of peace while the enemy is still far away. ³³ So you cannot become my disciple without giving up everything you own."

Jesus Teaches About Building on a Solid Foundation

Matthew 7:24-27
24 "Anyone who listens to my teaching and follows it is wise, like a person who builds a house on solid rock. 25 Though the rain comes in torrents and the floodwaters rise and the winds beat against that house, it won't collapse because it is built on bedrock. 26 But anyone who hears my teaching and doesn't obey it is foolish, like a person who builds a house on sand. 27 When the rains and floods come and the winds beat against that house, it will collapse with a mighty crash."

Luke 6:47-49
47 I will show you what it's like when someone comes to me, listens to my teaching, and then follows it. 48 It is like a person building a house who digs deep and lays the foundation on solid rock. When the floodwaters rise and break against that house, it stands firm because it is well built. 49 But anyone who hears and doesn't obey is like a person who builds a house right on the ground, without a foundation. When the floods sweep down against that house, it will collapse into a heap of ruins.

"We pay a price not only for doing the right thing, but we also pay a price if we do the wrong thing. I submit to you that the price we pay for wrong choices is much greater and leaves us sorrowful and filled with regret and misery."
(Joyce Meyer, 2016)

Kerching

Jesus Tells the Parable of the Two Sons

Matthew 21:28-32

[28] "But what do you think about this? A man with two sons told the older boy, 'Son, go out and work in the vineyard today.' [29] The son answered, 'No, I won't go,' but later he changed his mind and went anyway. [30] Then the father told the other son, 'You go,' and he said, 'Yes, sir, I will.' But he didn't go. [31] "Which of the two obeyed his father?" They replied, "The first." Then Jesus explained his meaning: "I tell you the truth, corrupt tax collectors and prostitutes will get into the Kingdom of God before you do. [32] For John the Baptist came and showed you the right way to live, but you didn't believe him, while tax collectors and prostitutes did. And even when you saw this happening, you refused to believe him and repent of your sins.

"The hypocrite wants religion - even the Christian faith - only for the advantages he gains from it. He fails to truly turn his heart to God and do good to God's people. He carries Christ in his Bible, but not in his heart. He serves the devil while wearing the uniform of Christ."
(Tim Challies, 2017)

"A lot of this misunderstanding stems from our turning Christian evangelism into an emotional appeal followed by a "repeat this prayer after me" response. Instantly someone who hasn't really given Christianity much thought or counted its costs finds themselves on the inside. After they've already made the purchase, they're given a bill featuring all the things that their new, free faith is going to cost them. It's no wonder that they want to hold on to the religious perks and their personal preferences.

It's kind of amazing how many people in the first-century wanted to follow Jesus but were sent away frustrated. (Mark 10:17–27, Luke 9:57–62) I think we need to present Christianity in a way that encourages people wrestle with its claims and sacrifices. We're so set on getting people "saved" that we end up packaging the gospel with a complimentary set of Ginsu knives—anything to get them to buy now. Unfortunately, Jesus encouraged us to make disciples, not just "save" people. (Matt. 28:16-20)"

(Jayson D. Bradley, 2016)

Have you truly counted the cost of following Jesus?

Piggy Bank

Thoughts on Discipleship

"It has become popular to preach a painless Christianity and automatic saintliness. It has become part of our "instant" culture. "Just pour a little water on it, stir mildly, pick up a gospel tract, and you are on your Christian way."
(A.W.Tozer, 2009)

"Discipleship is about how we live; not just the decisions we make, not just the things we believe, but a state of being."
(Rowan Williams, 2016)

"It is true that God may have called you to be exactly where you are. But, it is absolutely vital to grasp that he didn't call you there so you could settle in and live your life in comfort and superficial peace."
(Francis Chan, 2009)

"God deliberately chooses imperfect vessels — those who have been wounded, those with physical or emotional limitations. Then he prepares them to serve and sends them out with their weakness still in evidence, so that his strength can be made perfect in that weakness."
(Christine Caine, 2012)

"The ego hates losing – even to God."
(Richard Rohr, 2012)

'Therefore, this is what the Sovereign Lord says: "Look! I am placing a foundation stone in Jerusalem, a firm and tested stone. It is a precious cornerstone that is safe to build on. Whoever believes need never be shaken."'
Isaiah 28:16

Father, I'm sorry I sometimes treat living for You like a takeaway menu: picking and choosing the bits of me that You get to have control over. There have been times when I've wanted to give You everything, especially when things get tough and I'm struggling to find my way. But I've been too scared of what You might want in return. And when I do finally give You my all, I'm pretty sure I start taking it back, bit by bit, almost straight away. I do want to build my life on and in You - the solid rock, the Cornerstone. So give me strength Lord, to obey You. Touch my heart, mind and soul and let me truly understand just how wide, long, high and deep Your love for me is. Because knowing that each and every day inside the very heart of me means I can't give you anything less.
(Alex Mortimer, 2017)

Thirsty?

The following music tracks can be used to provide additional refreshment during your meal.
The House You're Building - Audrey Assad
Build This House - Lou Fellingham

Tic Toc

Tic Toc

The bags of silver had been handed out, the time had passed and now the three servants stood before their master. After a long and tiring trip, he was keen to see the return on his investment. How had the three servants used the gift they had been given? Had they invested it wisely so that it could flourish and grow, or had they buried it away out of fear that it had no real value? Surely none of his servants would do something like that. Now was the time to find out!
We are gifted with time, talents, money and relationships and yet sometimes we forget the source of all these blessings. We hide and discredit talents that we have been given while fearing what others will think. God's love for us is not dependent on the things we do, but one day He'll want to ask us what we did with His investment.

Today's Special

"So whether you eat or drink, or whatever you do,
do it all for the glory of God."
1 Corinthians 10:31

The Way We Invest Our Time & Talents

Jesus Tells the Parable of the Loaned Money

Matthew 25:14-30

[14] "Again, the Kingdom of Heaven can be illustrated by the story of a man going on a long trip. He called together his servants and entrusted his money to them while he was gone. [15] He gave five bags of silver to one, two bags of silver to another, and one bag of silver to the last—dividing it in proportion to their abilities. He then left on his trip. [16] "The servant who received the five bags of silver began to invest the money and earned five more. [17] The servant with two bags of silver also went to work and earned two more. [18] But the servant who received the one bag of silver dug a hole in the ground and hid the master's money.

[19] "After a long time their master returned from his trip and called them to give an account of how they had used his money. [20] The servant to whom he had entrusted the five bags of silver came forward with five more and said, 'Master, you gave me five bags of silver to invest, and I have earned five more.' [21] "The master was full of praise. 'Well done, my good and faithful servant. You have been faithful in handling this small amount, so now I will give you many more responsibilities. Let's celebrate together!'

[22] "The servant who had received the two bags of silver came forward and said, 'Master, you gave me two bags of silver to invest, and I have earned two more.'
[23] "The master said, 'Well done, my good and faithful servant. You have been faithful in handling this small amount, so now I will give you many more responsibilities. Let's celebrate together!'
[24] "Then the servant with the one bag of silver came and said, 'Master, I knew you were a harsh man, harvesting crops you didn't plant and gathering crops you didn't cultivate. [25] I was afraid I would lose your money, so I hid it in the earth. Look, here is your money back.'
[26] "But the master replied, 'You wicked and lazy servant! If you knew I harvested crops I didn't plant and gathered crops I didn't cultivate, [27] why didn't you deposit my money in the bank? At least I could have gotten some interest on it.'
[28] "Then he ordered, 'Take the money from this servant, and give it to the one with the ten bags of silver. [29] To those who use well what they are given, even more will be given, and they will have an abundance. But from those who do nothing, even what little they have will be taken away. [30] Now throw this useless servant into outer darkness, where there will be weeping and gnashing of teeth.'

"Crazy busy is life without peace. It's marked by decisions made for the approval of the world, not the approval of God"

(Alli Worthington, 2016)

Jesus Teaches About Salt and Light

Matthew 5:13-16
[13] "You are the salt of the earth. But what good is salt if it has lost its flavour? Can you make it salty again? It will be thrown out and trampled underfoot as worthless.
[14] "You are the light of the world—like a city on a hilltop that cannot be hidden. [15] No one lights a lamp and then puts it under a basket. Instead, a lamp is placed on a stand, where it gives light to everyone in the house. [16] In the same way, let your good deeds shine out for all to see, so that everyone will praise your heavenly Father.

The Parable of the Barren Fig Tree

Luke 13:6-9
[6] Then Jesus told this story: "A man planted a fig tree in his garden and came again and again to see if there was any fruit on it, but he was always disappointed. [7] Finally, he said to his gardener, 'I've waited three years, and there hasn't been a single fig! Cut it down. It's just taking up space in the garden.'
[8] "The gardener answered, 'Sir, give it one more chance. Leave it another year, and I'll give it special attention and plenty of fertiliser.
[9] If we get figs next year, fine. If not, then you can cut it down.'"

> "There is no perfect decision - only the perfectly surrendered decision to press through our fears and know that God is working in us to bring about good through us."
> (Lysa Terkeurst, 2014)

Tic Toc

We were made to produce fruit, not simply take up space in the garden.

Bags of Silver

Abilities

Characteristics

Tic Toc

Opportunities

Tic Toc

"That was a season when it was kind of all open, waiting to be re-created, each on the cusp of something, but we didn't know that. So we talked about how God made each of us, what we're good at, what we're not, what we might do, what we never will. Sometimes we get so tangled up in our own perceptions of ourselves that we lose perspective, seeing only our failures and bad habits. In difficult seasons, it's almost impossible to remember that feeling of being great at something or being proud of yourself.
We reminded one another that night, and we dreamed on behalf of one another. Left to our own devices, we sometimes choose the most locked up, dark versions of the story, but a good friend turns on the lights, opens the window, and reminds us that there are a whole lot of ways to tell the same story."
(Shauna Niequist, 2015)

"Our deepest fear is not that we are inadequate. Our deepest fear is that we are powerful beyond measure. It is our light, not our darkness that most frightens us. We ask ourselves, Who am I to be brilliant, gorgeous, talented, fabulous? Actually, who are you not to be? You are a child of God. Your playing small does not serve the world.
There is nothing enlightened about shrinking so that other people won't feel insecure around you. We are all meant to shine, as children do. We were born to make manifest the glory of God that is within us. It's not just in some of us; it's in everyone. And as we let our own light shine, we unconsciously give other people permission to do the same.
As we are liberated from our own fear, our presence automatically liberates others."
(Marianne Williamson, 2015)

'For we are God's masterpiece. He has created us new in Christ Jesus, so we can do the good things he planned for us long ago.'
Ephesians 2:10

Father, thank you! You have created me - wonderfully and fearfully made me - for Your purpose. How can that be? Why me? Forgive my doubts and questions but speak again into my heart so I can hold on to Your promises in my life. Holy Spirit, I want all that I am and all that I have to be Yours. Forgive me when I stumble or stop, but speak into my heart again and give me strength and stamina. Guide me and guard me so that my time and talents are truly yours.
(Alex Mortimer, 2017)

Thirsty?

The following music tracks can be used to provide additional refreshment during your meal.
I Surrender All (All to Jesus) - Casting Crowns
Brave - Nichole Nordeman

Tweet !?

Tweet

Tweet

The widow had been there many times before, standing in the doorway of the judge who was meant to protect her. Since her husband had passed away she had repeatedly called on the judge to listen and give her the justice she deserved. His cruel heart had turned her away. She made a choice. There would be no twittering on to friends about her dilemma and no one would stand before the judge instead of her. She would be persistent. She would be relentless. No matter what, she would make him listen to her.

If, through persistent requests for help, a cruel hearted judge was able to meet the needs of a widow, then surely a loving God is ready and waiting to do the same for us. He is longing to give us the love, security, justice and peace that we so desperately want.
We just need to ask for it!

Today's Special

"Don't worry about anything; instead, pray about everything. Tell God what you need, thank him for all he has done."
Philippians 4:6

The Importance of Prayer
Jesus Tells the Parable of the Persistent Widow

Luke 18:1-8

¹ One day Jesus told his disciples a story to show that they should always pray and never give up. ² "There was a judge in a certain city," he said, "who neither feared God nor cared about people. ³ A widow of that city came to him repeatedly, saying, 'Give me justice in this dispute with my enemy.' ⁴ The judge ignored her for a while, but finally he said to himself, 'I don't fear God or care about people, ⁵ but this woman is driving me crazy. I'm going to see that she gets justice, because she is wearing me out with her constant requests!'" ⁶ Then the Lord said, "Learn a lesson from this unjust judge. ⁷ Even he rendered a just decision in the end. So don't you think God will surely give justice to his chosen people who cry out to him day and night? Will he keep putting them off? ⁸ I tell you, he will grant justice to them quickly! But when the Son of Man returns, how many will he find on the earth who have faith?"

Jesus Tells the Parable of the Two Men Who Prayed

Luke 18:9-14

⁹ Then Jesus told this story to some who had great confidence in their own righteousness and scorned everyone else: ¹⁰ "Two men went to the Temple to pray. One was a Pharisee, and the other was a despised tax collector. ¹¹ The Pharisee stood by himself and prayed this prayer: 'I thank you, God, that I am not like other people—cheaters, sinners, adulterers. I'm certainly not like that tax collector! ¹² I fast twice a week, and I give you a tenth of my income.' ¹³ "But the tax collector stood at a distance and dared not even lift his eyes to heaven as he prayed. Instead, he beat his chest in sorrow, saying, 'O God, be merciful to me, for I am a sinner.' ¹⁴ I tell you, this sinner, not the Pharisee, returned home justified before God. For those who exalt themselves will be humbled, and those who humble themselves will be exalted."

Tweet

"The prerequisite for receiving the grace of God is to know you need it."
(Timothy Keller, 2009)

And when you pray...

Using the framework of the Lord's Prayer,
write your own version relating to your own experience.

"Our Father in heaven, Reveal who you are.
Set the world right; Do what's best - as above, so below.
Keep us alive with three square meals.
Keep us forgiven with you and forgiving others.
Keep us safe from ourselves and the Devil.
You're in charge! You can do anything you want!
You're ablaze in beauty! Yes. Yes. Yes."
Matthew 6:9-13(MSG)

"Our Father in heaven, help us to honour your name.
Come and set up your kingdom, so that everyone on earth
will obey you, as you are obeyed in heaven.
Give us our food for today.
Forgive us for doing wrong, as we forgive others.
Keep us from being tempted and protect us from evil."
Matthew 6:9-13(CEV)

Prayer Quotes

"One of the great uses of Twitter and Facebook will be to prove at the Last Day that prayerlessness was not from lack of time."
(John Piper, 2009)

"Is prayer your steering wheel or your spare tyre?"
(Corrie Ten Boom)

"Our prayers may be awkward. Our attempts may be feeble. But since the power of prayer is in the one who hears it and not in the one who says it, our prayers do make a difference."
(Max Lucado, 2017)

"The reality is, my prayers don't change God. But, I am convinced prayer changes me. Praying boldly boots me out of that stale place of religious habit into authentic connection with God Himself."
(Lysa Terkeurst, 2014)

"The Christian life is not a constant high. I have my moments of deep discouragement. I have to go to God in prayer with tears in my eyes, and say, 'O God, forgive me,' or 'Help me.'"
(Billy Graham)

"You must pray with all your might. That does not mean saying your prayers, or sitting gazing about in church or chapel with eyes wide open while someone else says them for you. It means fervent, effectual, untiring wrestling with God. This kind of prayer be sure the devil and the world and your own indolent, unbelieving nature will oppose. They will pour water on this flame."
(William Booth)

"Rather than set aside daily time for prayer, I pray constantly and spontaneously about everything I encounter on a daily basis. When someone shares something with me, I'll often simply say, 'let's pray about this right now.'"
(Thomas Kinkade)

Scripture Search

Each of the following Bible verses contain a prayer. Find out who the prayer belongs to and the story behind the words that are written.

1 Chronicles 4:10

Luke 1:46-49

Luke 18:13

Habakkuk 3:2

Jonah 2:1-2

Luke 23:42

Psalm 25:1-2

2 Chronicles 14:11

1 Samuel 2:1-2

Ephesians 3:14-16

Tweet

Prayer should play an integral part of our everyday faith. It should be like breathing, a life-sustaining force seeing us through each day.

'Each morning You listen to my prayer, as I bring my
requests to You and wait for Your reply.'
Psalm 5:3

Every day Lord, I want to sing Your praises!
Every moment, I should speak of your goodness and mercy. You are
Creator, Saviour and Friend. Let my heart be filled with the knowledge
of Your power and authority so that I may worship You as You should
be, with adoration and awe. Calm my heart and mind - I shall not be
troubled for You are my Heavenly Father and You hear every whisper
and cry. All my thoughts and intentions are an open book to You.
Help me to fix my eyes on You alone and bring all things before You at all times.
(Alex Mortimer, 2017)

Thirsty?

The following music tracks can be used to provide additional refreshment during your meal.
Closer to Your Heart - Piano Prayer (Instrumental)
Sanctus Real - Prayer

Glug

Glug

He knew this was a big mistake, but the others were determined to stick with what they had always done. As they poured the new wine into the old goatskins, he continued to question the choice they were making, but they wouldn't listen. They liked the old goatskins. They were familiar, comfortable. He knew that the rich new wine, full of flavour and depth, would expand and grow refusing to stay contained within the old goatskin. He knew that the bag would break and the new wine would wash away. His only option was to do things differently and reach for a brand new goatskin.

God is doing a new thing in our hearts, in our churches, and in our world. As He pours new wine into our lives, are we reaching for the old goatskin or offering a new life for Him to fill?

Today's Special

"But forget all that - it is nothing compared to what I am going to do.
For I am about to do something new.
See, I have already begun! Do you not see it?
I will make a pathway through the wilderness.
I will create rivers in the dry wasteland."
Isaiah 43:18-19

Glug

The Capacity for Change
Religious Leaders Ask Jesus About Fasting

Matthew 9:14-17

¹⁴ One day the disciples of John the Baptist came to Jesus and asked him, "Why don't your disciples fast like we do and the Pharisees do?"
¹⁵ Jesus replied, "Do wedding guests mourn while celebrating with the groom? Of course not. But someday the groom will be taken away from them, and then they will fast.
¹⁶ "Besides, who would patch old clothing with new cloth? For the new patch would shrink and rip away from the old cloth, leaving an even bigger tear than before.
¹⁷ "And no one puts new wine into old wineskins. For the old skins would burst from the pressure, spilling the wine and ruining the skins. New wine is stored in new wineskins so that both are preserved."

Lub Dub

Glug

Blot

Kerching

Glug

Tic Toc

Tweet

Glug

Glug

'For behold, I create new heavens and new earth. The former things will not be remembered or come to mind.'
Isaiah 65:17-18

I have sat at Your feet Lord and heard Your teaching.
I pray that I can understand it, and You, better.
I want to live a life pleasing to You, full of wisdom, worship and praise. There are things I need to change; You have made me new and the old must be gone. Father, send Your Holy Spirit to help me continually be Yours, holding nothing back.
Make my heart new - full of love
Make my life new - full of devotion
Make my focus new - full of your glory
Make my schedule new - full of Your purpose
Make my resolve new - full of prayerful anticipation
(Alex Mortimer, 2017)

Thirsty?

Write Your Story - Francesca Battistelli
The Peace of God - Scripture Lullabies

For more information, our latest blog posts and other resources please visit www.soulwithaview.co.uk

Additional Dietary Requirements

Lub Dub

Macarthur, J. (2016). Parables. Nashville: Thomas Nelson.
Piano Prayer, (2017). King of My Heart: Piano Prayer
Shane and Shane, (2014). Open the Eyes of my Heart Lord. The Worship Initiative, Vol.2

Blot

Chan, F. & Yankoski, D. (2012). Crazy Love.
Cook, A. Gretzinger, S. (2015). Mercy. Bethel Music Publishing.
Lewis, C. (2012). The Screwtape letters. London: Collins.
Nordeman, N. Glover, B. & Garcia, D. (2017). Every Mile Mattered. Sparrow Records.
Warren, R. (2014) Forgiveness vs. Restoration of Trust. 21 May 2014 (Accessed 12th July 2016)

Kerching

Assad, A & Glover, B, (2010). The House You're Building. Sparrow Records
Bradley, J.D. (2016). Coming to Grips with Christian Hypocrisy. 5th April 2016 (Accessed 12th May 2017)
Busbee, M. Fellingham, L. & Fellingham N. (2005). Build Your House. Thankyou Music/The Livingstone Collective
Caine, C. (2012). Undaunted. Grand Rapids, Mich: Zondervan.
Challies, T. (2017). 5 Warnings to Those Who Merely Pretend to be Godly. 25th May 2017 (Accessed 1st July 2017)
Chan, F. (2009). Forgotten God: Reversing Our Tragic Neglect of the Holy Spirit. David C. Cook
Meyer, J. (2016). Seize the Day. Hodder & Stoughton
Rohr, R, (2012). Falling Upward. SPCK Publishing
Tozer, A.W. (2009). Jesus, Author of Our Faith. Moody Publishing
Williams, R. (2016). Being Disciples: Essentials of the Christian life. SPCK.

Tic Toc

Niequist, S. (2015). Savor. Zondervan
Nordeman, N. (2005). Brave. Sparrow Records
Terkeurst, L. (2014). The Best Yes. Thomas Nelson
Wheeler, J. DeVenter, V. & Hall, M. (2013) I Surrender All (All to Jesus), Provident Label Group LLC.
Williamson, M. (2015). A Return to Love: Reflections on the Principles of a "Course in Miracles." Harper Thorsons
Worthington, A. (2016). Breaking busy: How to Find Peace and Purpose in a World of Crazy. Zondervan.

Tweet

Booth, W. (n.d.). AZQuotes.com. Retrieved April 16, 2018, from AZQuotes.com
Graham, B. Quotes. (n.d.). BrainyQuote.com. Retrieved April 16, 2018, from BrainyQuote.com
Hammitt, M. Rohman, C. & Stevens, C. (2013). Pray. Sparrow
Kinkade, T. Quotes. (n.d.). BrainyQuote.com. Retrieved April 16, 2018, from BrainyQuote.com
Keller, T. (2009). The Prodigal God. Zondervan
Lucado, M. "Our prayers may be awkward. Our attempts may be feeble. But since the power of prayer is in the one who hears it and not in the one who says it, our prayers do make difference." 7th July 2017. 7:00AM Tweet
Piano Prayer. (2017). Closer to Your Heart: Piano Prayer
Piper, J. "One of the great uses of Twitter and Facebook will be to prove at the Last Day that prayerlessness was not from lack of time." 20th October 2009. 2:02PM. Tweet
TerKeurst, L. (2014). I'm Scared to Pray Boldy. Proverbs 31 Ministries 27th February 2014 (Accessed 1st June 2017)
Ten Boom, C. (n.d.). BrainyQuote.com. Retrieved April 16, 2018, from BrainyQuote.com
William Booth. (n.d.). AZQuotes.com. Retrieved April 16, 2018, from AZQuotes.com

Glug

Battistelli, F. Glover,B. & Garcia, D. (2014). Write Your Story. Word, F.
Stocker, J. 2009. The Peace of God. Scripture Lullabies

For more information, our latest blog posts and other resources please visit www.soulwithaview.co.uk

www.ingramcontent.com/pod-product-compliance
Lightning Source LLC
Chambersburg PA
CBHW040325300426
44112CB00021B/2881